River Plants

Ernestine Giesecke

Heinemann Library
Chicago, Illinois

©1999 Reed Educational & Professional Publishing
Published by Heinemann Library,
an imprint of Reed Educational & Professional Publishing.
Chicago, Illinois
Customer service 888-454-2279
Visit our website at www.heinemannlibrary.com

 Designed by Depke Design
Illustrations by Eileen Mueller Neill
Printed in Hong Kong by South China Printing Co. (1988) Ltd.

03 02
10 9 8 7 6 5 4 3 2

Library of Congress Cataloging-in-Publication Data

Giesecke, Ernestine, 1945-
    River plants / Ernestine Giesecke.
      p. cm. – (Plants)
    Includes bibliographical references (p.) and index.
    Summary: Describes how various plants adapt to life alongside a river, including the fern, yellow flag iris, and glasswort.
    ISBN 1-57572-827-3 (lib. bdg.)   1-4034-0531-X (pbk. bdg.)
    1. Stream plants—Juvenile literature. [1. Stream plants.]
I. Title. II. Series: Plants (Des Plaines, Ill.)
QK932.7.G54   1999
581.76'4—dc21   98-45521
                         CIP
                         AC

Acknowledgments:

The Publisher would like to thank the following for permission to reproduce photographs:
Cover: Phil Degginger/Dr. E.R. Degginger
Phil Degginger/Dr. E.R. Degginger pp. 4-5; Ralph A. Reinheld/Earth Scenes p. 8; Breck P. Kent/Earth Scenes p. 9; John Stern/Animals Animals p. 10; Donald Specker/Earth Scenes p. 11; Dr. E.R. Degginger pp. 12, 16, 18, 22-23; R.J. Erwin/Photo Researchers, Inc. p. 14-15; Nancy M. Wells/Visuals Unlimited p. 17; John Sohlden/Visuals Unlimited p. 19; Robert Maier/Earth Scenes p. 20; Jack Wilburn/Earth Scenes p. 24; C C Lockwood/Earth Scenes p. 25; Robert Bornemann/Photo Researchers, Inc. pp. 26-27; Alan L. Detrick/Dr. E.R. Degginger p. 28.

Some words are shown in bold, **like this.** You can find out what they mean by looking in the glossary.

CAUTION!
Always take an adult with you when you explore a river. Be careful along the river bank. It may be slippery or steep—easy to fall into but hard to climb out of.

Contents

The River

A river is a moving body of water. A river usually begins in a high area like a hill or mountain. As it moves, the river carves a path in the earth. A **bank** forms on each side of the river.

Small rivers empty into larger rivers.
Eventually, the large river empties into
the ocean.

River Plants

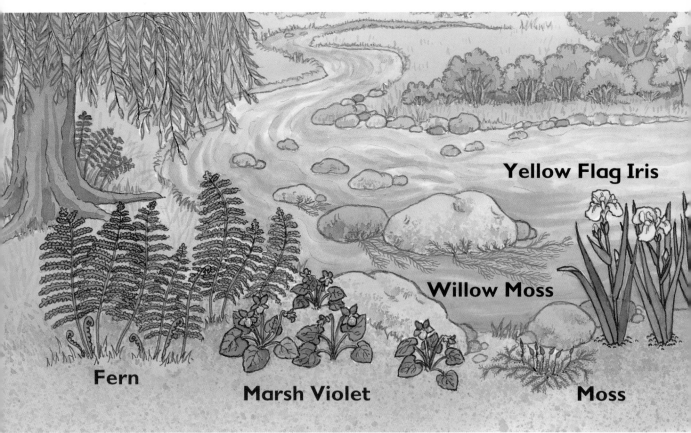

Yellow Flag Iris

Willow Moss

Fern

Marsh Violet

Moss

Different plants grow in different places along a river. Some plants grow in the shallow waters where the river begins.

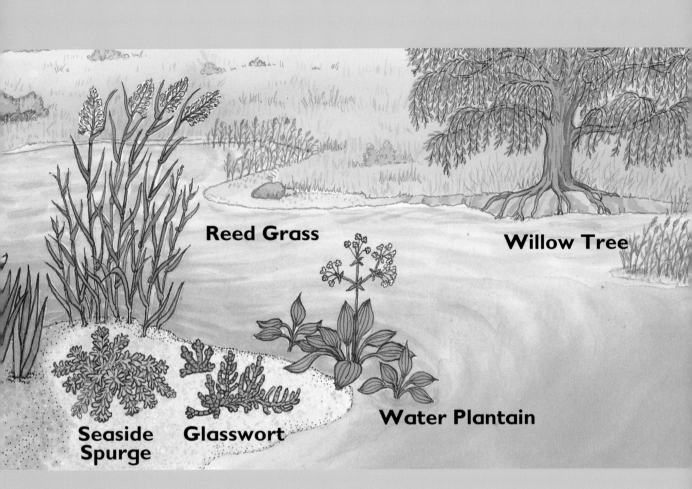

Reed Grass

Willow Tree

Water Plantain

Seaside Spurge

Glasswort

Other plants grow along the river **banks**.
Some grow best where the river meets the
sea. Because the water is always moving,
few plants grow in the river.

Moss

Mosses often form thick mats or carpets. They grow in places that are wet most of the time. They usually grow in shade.

Mosses have something like a flat leaf that grows from the stem. Mosses do not have roots. They soak up the **nutrients** they need from the water around them.

Fern

The leafy part of this fern is called a
frond. Some fern fronds may grow
underground for two years before they
appear above the **soil.**

A fern plant does not use flowers to **reproduce.** The brown **spores** on this fern will eventually grow into new ferns.

Marsh Violet

This marsh violet has heart-shaped leaves.
The roots of the violet trap **soil** and mud
along the river **bank**. Very tiny animals
live in the mud near the plant stems.

The marsh violet has a pretty
blue flower. It is on a stem that lifts the
flower above the leaves of the plant.

Willow Moss

This willow moss has root-like threads called **holdfasts**. It uses them to cling to a log in the river or a rock on the river **bank.** The willow moss does not need roots. It gets its **nutrients** through its leaves.

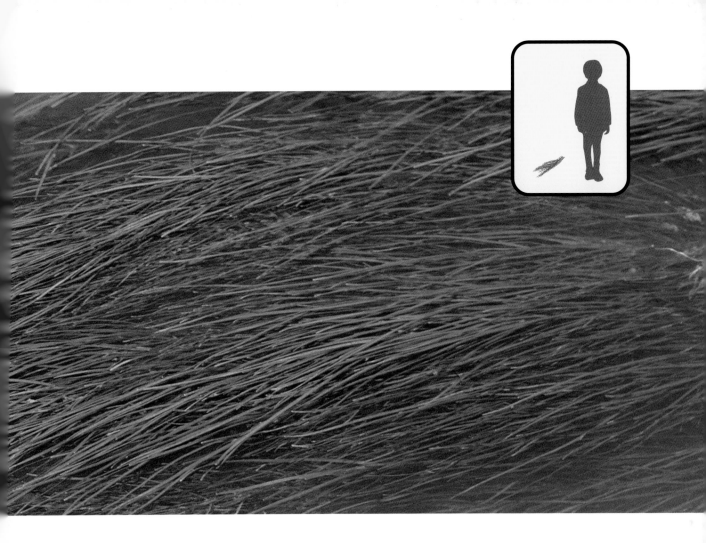

Even though willow moss clings to the
log, it can sway back and forth with the
moving water. Many small animals can
hide in the willow moss.

Reed Grass

Reeds grow along some river **banks.** The roots and stems of reeds creep along the river bank. They hold the plant in place. They also hold the river bank together.

A reed has a round, hollow stem like a drinking straw. Some birds build their nests in reeds along river banks.

Water Plantain

Water plantain has roots in the mud
along the **banks** of small rivers and
streams. Another name for the plant is
arrowhead because the leaves are
shaped like arrows.

When the water plantain blooms you can see tiny purple flowers. Sometimes plantains are called duck potatoes because ducks eat the plant's **tubers.**

Yellow Flag Iris

The yellow flag iris is a tall thin plant that grows on the river **bank**. Its long leaves grow up from the thick underground stem of the plant.

Some birds hide in the leaves of the yellow flag iris. The leaves also provide food for small animals that live near the river.

Willow Tree

Willow trees needs lots of water. They often grow along the **banks** of rivers and streams. The willow tree's **catkins** fall from the tree branches into the river.

The river's **current** will carry the seeds from the willow tree **downstream.** Eventually the seeds will take root in river bank mud.

Glasswort

Some places along the mouth of the river are sheltered and salty. This glasswort is one of the few plants that can grow in salty areas.

The glasswort has delicate roots to hold it in place. Its thick leaves and stem help it store water and keep it from drying out.

Seaside Spurge

Seaside spurge grows in the small hills of sand at the mouth of the river. Its roots help to hold the sand and **soil** in place.

The seaside spurge has thick leaves.
This helps them keep from drying out
in the harsh sun and salty sea water.

The River's Future

Sometimes cities and towns dump garbage into nearby rivers. Some factories pour dirty waste water into other rivers. The dirty water mixes with clean water to make the whole river unclean.

When this happens, the plants and animals that depend on the river cannot live. Soon the river itself dies. You can do your part to save a river. Never throw garbage or dump dirty liquids in a river.

Glossary

bank   the rising ground on either side of a river

catkin   a long, slender, line of flowers

current   the water that is moving in a river

downstream   direction of the water movement in a river

frond   leafy part of a fern

holdfasts   root-like threads that hold some plants in place

nutrients   things plants need to grow

reproduce   make new plants

soil   the ground that plants grow in

spore   part of some plants capable of making new plants

tubers   thick underground part of some plants

Parts of a Plant

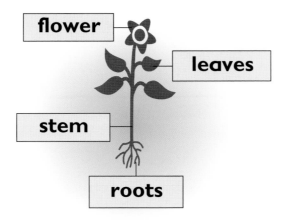

flower

leaves

stem

roots

More Books to Read

Fleisher, Paul. *Mountain Stream.* Tarrytown, NY: Marshall Cavendish Corporation. 1998. An older reader can help you with this book.

Fowler, Allan. *All Along the River.* Danbury, CT: Franklin Watts. 1998.

Llamas, Andreu. *The Vegetation of Rivers, Lakes, & Swamps.* Broomall, PA: Chelsea House Publishers. 1996. An older reader can help you with this book.

Morris, Neil. *Rivers & Lakes.* New York: Crabtree Publishing Company. 1998.

Pluckrose, Henry. *Flowers.* Danbury, CT: Children's Press. 1994.

Index